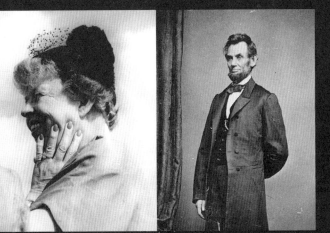

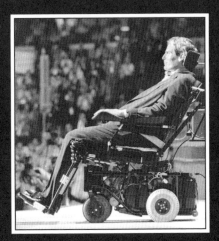

To: _____

A gift from: _____

HEROES FOR MY DAUGHTER

HARPER

An Imprint of HarperCollins*Publishers*

www.harpercollins.com

HEROES FOR MY

Daughter

BRAD MELTZER

HarperCollins books may be purchased for educational, business, or sales promotional use. For information, please e-mail the Special Markets Department at SPsales@harpercollins.com.

Designed by Fritz Metsch

Library of Congress Cataloging-in-Publication Data is available upon request.

ISBN: 978-0-06-190526-1

15 16 OV/RRD 10 9 8 7 6

For Lila,

MY DAUGHTER,

MY HERO

CONTENTS

ACKNOWLEDGMENTS

I have many heroes. But my favorite ones are always my little ones—my children—Jonas, Lila, and Theo, who are the three reasons this book exists. They inspire me, humble me, and forever remind me what true love is. My other hero is the woman who gave them to me: my wife, Cori, who is absolute proof that mothers are the greatest heroes. On that note, this book only exists because of the work of my own mother, Teri Meltzer. When I was younger, she used to tell me that she'd saw off her own arm for me. Yes, she had a gift for overstating things, but she meant it. My mom gave me everything she had and is the foundation of all I've become. It is in her memory that this book lives. Special love to my father, Stewie Meltzer, and my grandparents, Ben and Dotty Rubin, in whose memory this book was also completed. Also, a thank-you to my sister Bari for being a great aunt and for being there for me, and to Noah Kuttler for always, always pushing me so hard, especially with this one.

As I started writing this book, it became one of the most personal things I've ever worked on. And that is thanks to Jill Kneerim, who made sure that every page was all about my daughter Lila and my love for her. Special thanks also to Hope Denekamp, Caroline Zimmerman, and everyone at the Kneerim & Williams Agency; my treasured friend Larry Kirshbaum, the true godfather of this project; Simon Sinek, who told me my first inspiring story; Joel Marlin, who added the first pieces of research; Marie Grunbeck, for being me; Katherine Blood and Jonathan Eaker from the Library of Congress; Jason Sherry, who made it all move; Chris Weiss, who inspired so much of this; my friend Goody Marshall, who's been there from book one; Bill Morrison, Jeff Zaslow, and the nice people of The Christopher & Dana Reeve Foundation, as well as the National Portrait Gallery; Bob Miller, who put down the first brick of this house; Rob Weisbach, who had faith before anyone; and all the real heroes who shared pictures and family stories.

A personal thank-you must also be said to my alter ego, Brad Desnoyer, who understands me like no one else. This house was built on his research. And while I love his help, what means far more is his friendship. Also thanks to the amazing Nick Marell. Without his hard work and photo-finding, there'd be nothing to look at.

Finally, a thank-you to the wonderful Kathryn Whitenight, Tina Andreadis, Kathy Schneider, Katie O'Callaghan, Cindy Achar, Lydia Weaver, Doug Jones, Katie Salisbury, and everyone at HarperCollins, for giving this book such a beautiful home. And to Jonathan Burnham, whose graciousness and help will always be appreciated. Thank you, Jonathan, for this gift for my daughter—and for your faith.

INTRODUCTION

*D*ear Lila, my sweet daughter,

I love you. And yes, I know every parent loves their child. But not like I love you. Someday, you'll roll your eyes and groan, "Dad, you're *embarrassing* me." But right now, you're only six years old, so these days, you still smile your big beaming smile when I say things like that. And I point that out simply so that, when these days are gone, I'll have proof they existed.

On the day you were born, I remember your mom waking up at four o'clock in the morning, rolling over in bed, and telling me, "I think the baby's coming."

"Go back to bed," I pleaded. "It's too early."

God bless your mother, she actually tried to go back to bed.

But you—my little unborn daughter—had your own ideas. Believe me when I say that wouldn't be the last time.

At the hospital, the instant I saw you, my heart doubled in size. My own mother, your grandmother, told me at the time, "Now you'll understand how I love you."

After giving us a few moments with you, the nurses did their usual weighing and measuring, and then said they wanted to whisk you off for your first bath.

"I'm coming with you," I told them, determined to protect you.

They smiled that smile they save for new parents and reassured me, "She'll be fine. We have her."

But as I looked down at my beautiful, teeny, amazing daughter . . . C'mon . . . No way was I ever letting you out of my sight. *I had to protect you!* Thankfully, the nurses put up with me, and let me pretend I was some old parental veteran as I helped give you your first bath. Later, as I sat there, rocking in the rocking chair they gave me and holding you close, I still remember all the dreams I was dreaming for you.

I didn't want just *one* thing for you. I wanted *everything*. If you needed strength, I wanted you to be strong. If you saw someone hurting, I wanted you to find the compassion to help. If there was a problem, big or small, that no one could solve, I wanted you to have every available skill—ingenuity, empathy, creativity, perseverance—so you could attack that problem in a way that no one else on this entire planet had ever fathomed. And that would be your greatest gift, Lila: That *no one*—and I mean *no one*—would ever be exactly *you*.

I still believe that. I do. I'm a mushy dad. And it was in those first moments of blind idealism and unbridled naïveté that I resolved to write a book for you.

That very night—six years ago, on the night you were born—I went home and started this book. My goal was to write it over the course of your life. I'd fill it with all the advice you needed to be a good person. I began the list that night:

1. Love God.
2. Help the kids who need it.

My plan was to add more ideas as you grew older, and eventually, on the day when I presented this book to you, you'd realize I was *indeed* the greatest father of all time (I had a parade planned for myself as well).

Thankfully, during your first few years, I realized my clichéd, self-important plan was just that. It hit me after hearing the stories of heroes like Sally Ride. Sure, I knew she was the first American woman to travel into space. But at a time when there were no women astronauts, do you know why NASA chose her? Some say it was because she was a genius at physics . . . or that it was her physical resolve and athletic ability . . . or that she was simply fearless. And sure, it was probably *all* those things. But it was also because when she saw an ad in her college's newspaper looking for female astronauts, Sally Ride saw an opportunity. And grabbed it. In that moment, she dared to attempt what no woman had done before.

I *love* that story. I wanted *you* to hear that story. I wanted your brothers to hear that story. I wanted everyone in this world to know that if you take a chance . . . and work hard . . . you can do anything in this world.

Soon after, my new plan was born. I wouldn't give you a book of *rules*. I'd give you a book of *heroes*. And in that, I'd give you absolute proof that anything is possible.

When you're older, this will be the point where you'll again roll your eyes and again groan, *"Dad, did you just tell me 'anything is possible?' You're embarrassing me. Again."* I won't begrudge you, Lila. I did the same thing. But let me be clear: My dreams for you today are different from the ones on the day you were born. Sure, I still want everything for you. I always will. But amongst those dreams, there's one I keep coming back to. It's the dream that links every single hero in these pages. You'll see inside when you read it, my daughter. Every hero in here is a fighter. And Lila, no matter what stage of life you're in, when you want something—no matter how impossible it seems—you need to *fight for it*. When you believe in something, *fight for it*. And when you see injustice, fight harder than you've ever fought before.

To see the results, read the story of Marie Curie, who never stopped pushing science forward, even when she was dying from the radiation she was studying . . . or the story of Billie Jean King, who challenged (and beat!) the pig-headed man who told her that women were weaker than men.

Women are not weaker. Read that again, Lila. *Women are not weaker.* They are just as strong, just as resolute, just as creative, and are filled with just as much potential as any man. Yes, as your father, my instinct is to protect you (like that first day with the nurses). Other people will want to protect you too. But remember that you are not a damsel in distress, waiting for some prince to rescue you. Forget the prince. With your brain and your resourcefulness, you can rescue yourself. And when you have your doubts—as we all inevitably do—you'll have this book, full of people who were wracked with just as much fear, but who also found the internal strength to overcome it.

From Amelia Earhart to Abigail Adams to every person in here, you'll see the stories of women (and men) who are no different from you and me. We may lionize them and put them on pedestals. But never forget this: No one is born a hero. Every person in this book had moments where they were scared and terrified. Like you. Like me. So how did they achieve what they achieved? Because whatever their dreams were, big or small—for their country, for their family, or even for themselves—they never stopped fighting for what they loved.

We all are who we are—until that moment when we strive for something greater.

Is that schmaltzy and naïve? I hope so. Because I want you to learn those things too.

And so, my daughter, here is your book. This book is my dream for you. And it's a dream that was built by both myself and the most important hero of all: your mother. When you have doubts, there is strength inside. When you are ready to give up, there's motivation inside. And when you have questions, there are answers inside. But I hope you know, as every person in these pages proves, the best answers will always come from what's within you.

> I love you, my Lila-boo.
> Dad
> (aka Brad Meltzer)
> Fort Lauderdale, Florida 2011

HEROES FOR MY DAUGHTER

MARIE CURIE

Scientist. Researcher. Nobel Prize winner.

As one of history's greatest scientists, Marie Curie was awarded *two* Nobel Prizes—one for Physics and one for Chemistry. As a woman, however, she was not invited to address the audience at the acceptance ceremony. Today, her findings on radiation are part of the most complex protocols for treating people with cancer.

When she made her first revolutionary discovery, that radiation came from the interior of an atom, she could have stopped—she'd accomplished enough.

When she pushed her theory forward, inventing the term *radioactivity* to describe her findings, she could have stopped—she'd accomplished enough.

When she discovered two new elements, polonium and radium, and went on to become the first woman to win a Nobel Prize, she could have stopped—she'd accomplished enough.

And when her husband died and the French government offered her support in the form of a pension, Marie Curie refused the money, saying she could take care of her two daughters by herself. She did it by becoming the Sorbonne's first female lecturer and professor.

From there she went on to win her *second* Nobel Prize, this one in chemistry, making her the first person to receive Nobel Prizes in two fields. She became so famous that when she traveled to the White House, President Harding presented her with a key to a lead-lined box that held one gram of radium. Worth more than one hundred thousand dollars, the radium was a gift from the women of America, who collected the money so Curie could continue her groundbreaking research.

As she got older, Curie kept going, working with her daughter to find medical applications for her research. Indeed, even when she died from leukemia—after years of radiation exposure—we were still learning from her.

Throughout her life, with so much accomplished, she could have stopped, she could have stopped, she could have stopped.

Lucky for us, she didn't.

One never notices what has been done; one can only see what remains to be done. . . .
—MARIE CURIE

MALLORY HOLTMAN AND LIZ WALLACE

Softball players.

As players on Central Washington University's softball team, Mallory Holtman and Liz Wallace lost a game of baseball. And won the game of life.

Western Oregon University senior Sara Tucholsky had never hit a home run before—not in high school, not in college, not ever in her twenty-one years of playing softball.

But at this doubleheader, with hecklers yelling at her, Tucholsky smashed the ball over the center-field fence.

Amazed at her home run, Tucholsky forgot to touch first base.

As she quickly turned to correct the mistake, her knee blew out.

She had torn a ligament—her ACL.

Tucholsky was on the ground, crawling back to first.

Here's the key: If anyone from her team tried to help her, Tucholsky would be called out. The umpires said that if she couldn't continue beyond first base, and a pinch runner was put in, her over-the-fence hit would count only as a two-run single.

That's when the opposing team's first baseman, Mallory Holtman, said to an umpire, "Excuse me, would it be okay if we carried her around and she touched each bag?"

The umpires looked at each other.

What?

But as they discussed it, they realized there were no rules preventing the opposing side from helping.

So that's what Mallory and a teammate did.

Holtman and shortstop Liz Wallace literally carried Tucholsky—an opposing player—around the bases, making sure she tagged every base with her good left foot.

In the end, that home run contributed to Holtman and Wallace's team losing the game. It also meant that Holtman, a senior, would never make it into the NCAA playoffs.

Soon after, her softball career was over.

But there's a reason they now call Holtman the "greatest player" in her team's history. And it's not just because she's the all-time home run leader in her conference (which she is).

It was such a lesson that we learned—that it's not all about winning. And we forget that, because as coaches, we're always trying to get to the top. We forget that. But I will never, ever forget this moment. It's changed me, and I'm sure it's changed my players.

—PAM KNOX, coach for Western Oregon

JOAN GANZ COONEY

Helped create Sesame Street.

With the creation of *Sesame Street*, Joan Ganz Cooney changed the history of both television and education. Today, Big Bird, Oscar the Grouch, and Elmo reach over 100 million children in more than 140 countries.

At a dinner party, someone asked her, "Do you think television could be used to teach young children?"

Joan Ganz Cooney, who worked in TV, needed time to answer the question.

She started by commissioning a study.

The study offered a revolutionary conclusion.

And so began her experiment, which she called the Children's Television Workshop.

She hired researchers, writers, and artists.

And a young puppeteer named Jim Henson.

The first episode appeared in November 1969.

Forget commercials. This show was brought to you by the letters *W*, *S*, and *E*—and the numbers 2 and 3.

The cast was multicultural, so they looked like the preschoolers they wanted to help.

And of course, there was that big yellow bird who taught kids it was okay to make a few mistakes.

"Do you think television could be used to teach young children?"

Joan Ganz Cooney's answer was *Sesame Street.*

It was a resounding "Yes."

It's not whether children learn from television, it's what *children learn from television, because everything that children see on television is teaching them* something.

—JOAN GANZ COONEY

AUDREY HEPBURN

Actress. Ambassador. Relief worker.

Hollywood star Audrey Hepburn epitomized grace and beauty in films like *Breakfast at Tiffany's*. But despite being one of the few people to win an Oscar, a Tony, an Emmy, and a Grammy Award, her greatest role was as a UNICEF International Goodwill Ambassador, working to ensure no child would ever suffer through hunger.

As a child in Nazi-occupied Holland with nothing to eat, she nearly starved.

But as she witnessed her uncle's execution by firing squad, as she saw innocent families shipped off in trains, she knew others had it worse.

And when the liberation finally came—when the forerunner of a group called UNICEF brought her food and medical relief—she knew she was saved.

Forty years later, Audrey Hepburn was the greatest and most beautiful actress in the world.
She didn't have to do anything.
But that's when she reached out to UNICEF.
They didn't find her.
She found them.

From Ethiopia, to Turkey, to Sudan, to Bangladesh,
Audrey Hepburn made over fifty trips to the poorest and most desperate countries in the world, never forgetting her own near starvation as a child.

In 1992, just before she was diagnosed with cancer, she made her final visit—to Somalia.
Before President Clinton and later President George W. Bush sent troops, it was Audrey Hepburn who brought the tragedy there to the press and the world.
It is her greatest legacy:
Yes, the hunger that's in your belly can destroy you,
but the hunger that's in your soul—the hunger that drives you—
if you use it to help others,
it can be your greatest source of power.

Remember, if you ever need a helping hand, it's at the end of your arm. As you get older, remember you have another hand: the first is to help yourself, the second is to help others.
— AUDREY HEPBURN

Often the kids would have flies all over them, but she would just go hug them. I had never seen that. Other people had a certain amount of hesitation, but she would just grab them. Children would just come up to hold her hand, touch her—she was like the Pied Piper.
— JOHN ISAAC, chief of the UN Photo Unit

HELEN KELLER

Deaf. Blind. Limitless.

Helen Keller was the first deaf and blind person to earn a college degree. She would not be the last. Today, thousands of deaf and blind students enroll in universities—thanks to her work revolutionizing the education system and treatment of the blind, deaf, and mute.

When Helen was nineteen months old, an illness left her blind and deaf.
She didn't know how to read. Or even speak.
She hadn't yet learned language.
Now she was sealed in a black, silent place.
They said she'd never achieve anything.

But her teacher—Anne Sullivan—had faith in her.
Which inspired Helen to have faith in herself.

In the beginning, she had a few self-made signs.
Pushing meant "go." Pulling meant "come."
Anne taught her far more by finger-writing words into the palm of Helen's hand, which is how Helen learned language.

But when Helen felt the movements of Anne's mouth, she realized how most people communicated.
Immediately, Helen spelled, "I want to talk with my mouth."

Even her teacher was skeptical about teaching her.
It would've been so easy to let Helen keep signing, to let Anne be her voice . . .
But Anne had taught Helen too well. Now Helen wouldn't accept *easy*.

To feel the vibrations of each word, Helen put her thumb on Anne's throat,
her pointer finger on Anne's lips,
and her middle finger on Anne's nose.

At her seventh lesson, she spoke this sentence, word for word:
"I am not dumb now."

Oh, and that girl who they said would never achieve anything? She didn't just learn to speak English. She also became proficient in French and German.
And wrote twelve books.
And graduated from Radcliffe College at Harvard University.
Cum laude.

No pessimist ever discovered the secret of the stars or sailed an uncharted land, or opened a new doorway for the human spirit.
—HELEN KELLER

CHRISTOPHER REEVE

Actor. Activist for spinal cord research.

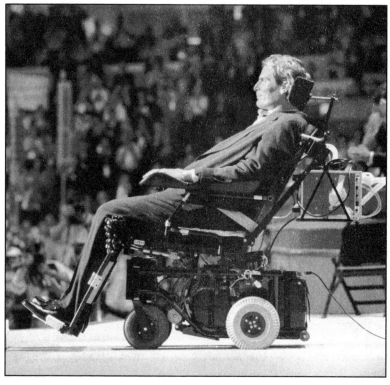

He was famous for playing Superman, but what made Christopher Reeve beloved happened after he was paralyzed in a riding accident. He spent the rest of his life as an advocate for spinal cord research and treatment.

Thrown from a horse, with his hands caught in the bridle, he landed *headfirst*.
In the hospital, as he lay there with his neck shattered, he told his wife, Dana, "Maybe we should let me go."
Without hesitation, Dana told him, "I'll be with you for the long haul, no matter what."
She then added the words that saved his life: "You're still you. And I love you."

The progress he made personally was nothing short of amazing, but what he did for others?
That was the miracle.
Despite his speech being slow and staccato,
despite his mobility being limited to a wheelchair controlled by a straw,
despite his independence being gone,
Christopher Reeve refused to stay down.

He lobbied Congress, fought for new research,
and even appeared on *Sesame Street* with Big Bird to explain how his wheelchair worked.

Despite what the doctors predicted, he was able to eventually move some of his fingers and regain sensation over much of his body.

People thought Christopher Reeve was Superman. He wasn't.
But he *was* Clark Kent.
Normal, vulnerable, and built just as fragile as the rest of us.
Thankfully, he never let that stop him.

When the first Superman movie came out, I was frequently asked, 'What is a hero?' My answer was that a hero is someone who commits a courageous action without considering the consequences. . . . Now my definition is completely different. I think a hero is an ordinary individual who finds the strength to persevere and endure in spite of overwhelming obstacles. They are the real heroes, and so are the families and friends who have stood by them.

—CHRISTOPHER REEVE

CAROL BURNETT

Actor. Funny lady. Woman of her word.

As the star and creator of *The Carol Burnett Show*, she was one of the funniest and most successful comedians in show business. Her show lasted eleven years, captured twenty-five Emmys, and was named one of *Time* magazine's 100 Best TV Shows of All Time.

After her father abandoned her and her mother's alcoholism became debilitating, Carol was raised by her grandmother in California. She grew up in poverty.

When she wanted to be an actress, she didn't have the money to go to New York.

That's when a secret benefactor came forward, willing to give her a thousand dollars to pursue her dream. The money came with three stipulations:

1. She could never reveal the donor's identity;
2. She had to repay the loan in five years; and
3. She had to help other young entertainers attain their dreams.

After working as a hat-check girl, Carol Burnett eventually found success and paid the loan back . . . five years to the day.

Then she set up an award to be given every year to a theater student at Emerson College. She could've stopped there.

Instead, she set up another award for theater students at UCLA.

Then she got a fan letter from a high school student, who wrote of her own dreams of working in show business.

Carol Burnett called the girl's house, went to see her perform at a local event, and eventually gave young Vicki Lawrence a starring role on her blockbuster TV show.

It's one thing to never forget where you came from.

But it's just as important to never forget who got you where you are today.

I've been helped by acts of kindness from strangers. That's why we're here, after all, to help others.
                                                      —CAROL BURNETT

Carol Burnett famously ended each show by tugging her ear, which was a secret greeting to the grandmother who raised her—the woman Carol forever loved.

AMELIA EARHART

Record breaker. High-flying pilot.

A pioneer in aviation and the first female to cross the Atlantic, Amelia Earhart broke many flight records. She died while trying to become the first person to fly around the world at the equator. Her plane has still never been found.

She worked as a truck driver, stenographer, and photographer. Just to save enough for the flying lessons.

Six months after she learned to fly, she put away enough for a bright yellow, used biplane called *Canary*.

The following year, she broke her first record, reaching an altitude of fourteen thousand feet, the highest recorded at that time by a woman.

She wasn't a natural. She wasn't the best pilot.

She had to work at it.

But within her short lifetime she showed the world that the greatest flight we'll ever take is the one no one has tried before.

Please know I am quite aware of the hazards. . . . I want to do it because I want to do it. Women must try to do things as men have tried. When they fail their failure must be but a challenge to others. —AMELIA EARHART

Never interrupt someone doing what you said couldn't be done. —AMELIA EARHART

ALEX SCOTT

Founder of Alex's Lemonade Stand.

∞

Eight-year-old Alex Scott opened what is arguably the most successful lemonade stand in history.

She was diagnosed with cancer before her first birthday.
It became the only life she knew: Sickness. Chemotherapy. Surgery.

When she was four, Alex asked to put a lemonade stand in her front yard.
It was her idea. Not her parents'. Hers.
She didn't do it to buy a new doll, or even pay hospital bills.
She told her parents she wanted to give the money to the doctors so they could find a cure for all the other children diagnosed with pediatric cancer.
Again, her idea.

In a single day, "Alex's Lemonade Stand" raised two thousand dollars.
Soon other stands began popping up—all with Alex's name on them.
Every year, Alex went back into the summer sun to sell her lemonade. And so did the others. Eventually, they raised two hundred thousand dollars.

For Alex, it wasn't enough. She had a new goal: one million dollars.

On June 12, 2004, hundreds of lemonade stands opened in every state across the country—ordinary people selling water, sugar, and lemons to raise money for kids with cancer.

Nearly two months later, Alex passed away while her parents held her hands. She was eight.
Make no mistake: the one-million-dollar goal was surpassed.
And before she died, Alex said the next year's goal should be *five million*.

Today, her dream has raised over $45 million. And it's still going.
One idea. One girl. One big dream.

Oh, we can do it. If other people will help me, I think we can do it. I know we can do it.
—ALEX SCOTT

ABIGAIL ADAMS

Wife. Mother. Patriot.

The wife of President John Adams and the mother of President John Quincy Adams, Abigail Adams was as outspoken as either of them in the new America she helped shape.

In April 1775, the shots were fired at Lexington and Concord—shots that started the American Revolution.

Within a month, with her husband away in the capital to help a struggling government, Abigail Adams turned her house into a sanctuary for colonial soldiers.

Her kitchen floor held all those who needed rest.
Her barn and attic became bedrooms for militiamen.
Her fireplace was used to melt spoons into ammunition.

All the while, she relayed the news to the person she called, "My Dearest Friend," reaffirming John Adams's belief that the American colonists had to fight for their liberty.

As the war went on, Abigail argued for women's rights and slaves' rights, and she did it at a time when, under English law, married women had no legal identity separate from their husbands.

In the letters she wrote to John Adams, and in her fight for equal rights, Abigail Adams made some of the boldest statements of her time.

So when history books talk about the Founding Fathers, let's not forget there were also Founding Mothers.

If we mean to have Heroes, Statesmen and Philosophers, we should have learned women.
—ABIGAIL ADAMS

ANNE FRANK

Author of The Diary of a Young Girl

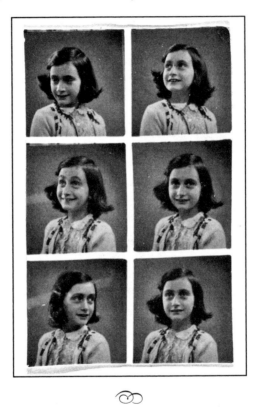

Forced to hide in an annex by the Nazi regime, teenager Anne Frank wrote her deepest thoughts in a simple diary. After Anne died in a Nazi concentration camp, her father published her diary and showed the world just how powerful a child's voice can be.

The rules changed slowly in Amsterdam.
First, her family's doors had to be locked by 8 p.m.
Then the police made her turn in her bicycle.

Yet even when she was forced to leave her school,
when her father was no longer allowed to drive,
when her mother could only buy groceries from stores marked "Jewish Shop,"
when her sister was ordered to report to a concentration camp,

Anne Frank still believed that people were good.

For two years and one month during World War II, as the Frank family hid in the annex
that was tucked behind a bookcase,
as she scribbled in that tiny book with the red-checked cover,
Anne Frank never gave up on humankind.

As a result, she gave the world the very best reason to *never forget*.

Think of all the beauty still left around you and be happy. —ANNE FRANK

DOROTHY DAY

Advocate for the poor and homeless.

After working with the poor during the Great Depression, Dorothy Day helped found the Catholic Worker movement, which led to the creation of hospitality houses and farming communes that are now all over the world. (© *Bob Fitch Photo*)

It started when she published a small newspaper about being hospitable to the homeless. Soon after, there was a knock on Dorothy's door—from a homeless woman seeking shelter.

To Dorothy it wasn't even a question. This was her mission.
She rented an apartment space for ten women, then another for men.
It grew in size, serving hundreds in New York.
Then her House of Hospitality spread across the country—thirty-three shelters that housed and fed the homeless, and asked nothing in return.

That was the one rule: Everyone—of every religion—was accepted.

Eventually, Mother Teresa came to visit *her* to pin a cross on Dorothy.

The Catholic Church has even recognized her as "a Servant of God"—the first step in officially making her a saint.

But of all her accomplishments, what mattered most was how she dealt with that first knock on the door.

In life, you will be faced with problems.

What counts is whether you turn away or tackle them.

The greatest challenge of the day is: how to bring about a revolution of the heart, a revolution which has to start with each one of us?   —DOROTHY DAY

JUDY BLUME

Bestselling author. Beloved storyteller.

In books like *Tales of a Fourth Grade Nothing*, Judy Blume trailblazed a new genre of books for young adults. Though critics have tried to censor her, her work has sold more than 80 million copies, in thirty-one languages.

They're called novels for a reason: they're supposed to carry with them something original, something new.

Some novels teach. Some entertain. Some comfort.

The best ones introduce ideas.

For more than four decades, Judy Blume has done just that, giving kids honest answers about their most complex questions—bras, sex, menstruation, puberty—and never talking down to them.

But at the end of the day, her most vital message is the one lesson all of us need to hear—at every age:
Whatever your quirks or idiosyncrasies, it is always okay to be exactly who you are.

Are you there God? It's me, Margaret. I just told my mother I want a bra. Please help me grow God. You know where. I want to be like everyone else.
—JUDY BLUME, *Are You There God? It's Me, Margaret*

SACAJAWEA

Explorer. Team member.

When explorers Lewis and Clark traversed the uncharted American West, the only woman on the five-thousand-mile journey was a Shoshone Indian named Sacajawea. She was only seventeen.

She was a pregnant teenager when her "husband" joined Lewis and Clark's Corps of Discovery.

But on this rough adventure,
where they'd face grizzly bears,
and eat candles to avoid starvation,
and nearly die from hail and flash flooding . . .
What good would it be for the expedition's leaders to have a teenage girl nursing a baby?

The question was answered almost immediately when, during a sudden storm, her husband lost control of the boat.

As the vessel nearly flipped, and the men panicked and fought, the supplies floated away.

Let me repeat that.

In the middle of the unknown wilderness, Lewis and Clark's supplies—which could not be replaced and were needed for them all to survive—were about to be lost.

But with her infant son strapped to her back, Sacajawea kept her cool.
Calmly balancing herself in the nearly capsized boat, she alone grabbed the items as they floated by.
It was this girl, this *young girl*, surrounded by soldiers and frontiersmen, who saved them all.

She didn't wait for someone to come to the rescue.
She came to the rescue.

Because of her resolve, when the men on the expedition later voted on where to camp the following winter, Sacajawea—the former hostage and slave—had a vote of equal value.

THEODORE ROOSEVELT

Rough Rider. Trustbuster. President.

As the youngest U.S. President in history, Theodore Roosevelt was well-known for his audacious style. He is the only person who has won both the Medal of Honor, which he won for war, and the Nobel Peace Prize.

It's called *chutzpah*.

You've seen it in our family: When someone acts with so much audacity, it almost seems ridiculous.

Teddy Roosevelt had chutzpah.

As President, he adopted the motto "Speak softly and carry a big stick," wielding that stick at injustices he saw.
As a trustbuster, he dismantled some of America's richest companies, refusing to let their dominance take advantage of others.
And as a Rough Rider in the Spanish-American War, he didn't just lead the charge up San Juan Hill—he campaigned for the Medal of Honor for getting there.

Chutzpah for sure.

But of all the battles Teddy Roosevelt boasted about, his greatest legacy was using the bully pulpit of the White House to protect something that couldn't protect itself: the environment.

As America's first conservationist President, Roosevelt established more than 100 million acres of national forest, five new national parks, and eighteen national monuments, including the historic Grand Canyon National Monument in Arizona.

How'd he do it?

Like this: When he heard that some Palm Beach yachtsmen were shooting brown pelicans for fun as the birds flew to their nests, he asked an aide, "Is there any law that will prevent me declaring Pelican Island a National Bird Sanctuary?"
"No," the aide replied.
"Very well, then," Roosevelt said, reaching for his pen. "I do declare it."

Chutzpah has its benefits.

Far better it is to dare mighty things, to win glorious triumphs, even though checkered by failure, than to take rank with those poor spirits who neither enjoy much nor suffer much, because they live in the gray twilight that knows neither victory nor defeat.

—TEDDY ROOSEVELT

JULIA CHILD

Passionate chef. Secret spy.

Although she began her career as a member of the secret OSS, the six-foot, two-inch Julia Child became the most famous, most recognized, most celebrated chef of our time by bringing French delicacies to the American dinner table. Her TV show, *The French Chef*, lasted from 1963 to 1973, with reruns still broadcast today.

She wasn't a natural cook.

When it came time for her final exam at France's famed cooking school, Julia Child failed.

She failed again when, after six years of working on her cookbook, her publisher rejected it. Total failure.

But she kept cooking.
She always kept cooking.

Eventually, a young editor at a different publishing house took the book home and actually tested one of Julia's recipes—boeuf bourguignon, to be exact. Soon a contract was on the way.

The book—*Mastering the Art of French Cooking*—became one of the most influential cookbooks of all time. And after its publication, the large, loud, and joyful Julia Child was given her own TV show.

Still, it all began with failure. And more failure. And more failure.

Luckily, Julia Child had one secret ingredient—the most vital ingredient of all: she never gave up.

That's how you make your masterpiece.

Find something you're passionate about and keep tremendously interested in it.
—Julia Child

GOLDA MEIR

Foreign minister. Prime minister.

Golda Meir dedicated her life to the foundation of the Jewish state of Israel. She served as Israel's first female prime minister.

Out of eight children, she was one of only three to survive past childhood.

No question, she was tough.

In school, she became valedictorian. At work, she always rose through the ranks.

No question, she was sharp—a natural leader.

And when dignitaries came to see Foreign Minister Meir, she would meet with them—on her terms—in her kitchen, where she would talk to them frankly about the importance of Israel's security.

No question, she was unlike anyone else.

But to understand how Golda Meir rose to become one of the few women to run a country—it all began with one relentless attribute:

Hard work.

When her cabinet chief said she should take a vacation, she asked, "Why? Do you think I'm tired?"
"No," he replied, "but I am."
Her response was quick: "So *you* take a vacation!"

Golda Meir didn't become a legend because she was a woman. She became a legend because she never stopped.

Whether women are better than men I cannot say . . . but I can say they are certainly no worse.
—GOLDA MEIR

STEVIE WONDER

Musical prodigy. Legendary singer-songwriter.

One of the most popular singers in the world, Stevie Wonder has won more Grammys than any other male artist. With songs like "You Are the Sunshine of My Life," he also proves that you don't have to see to believe in the goodness of humanity—you just have to listen.

Born premature, he weighed fewer than four pounds.
For fifty-two days, he fought inside an incubator.
The incubator saved his life. But the influx of oxygen had one additional effect:
It caused the baby to go blind.

By the time Stevie was three, there was one thing that was clear about this little blind boy.
He loved music.

By the time he was ten, he'd mastered the harmonica, piano, drums, and organ—without
ever having a lesson.
By eleven, he had a record deal with Motown.

So yes, I love that Stevie Wonder sings of tolerance and understanding.
And I love the fact that he used his song "Happy Birthday" as a rallying cry in the
campaign to make Martin Luther King Jr.'s birthday a national holiday.
But what I love most is that every time I hear "Isn't She Lovely,"
I think of you, my daughter.

Just because a man lacks the use of eyes doesn't mean he lacks vision.
—STEVIE WONDER

SUSAN B. ANTHONY

Advocate for giving women the right to vote.

In the later half of the nineteenth century, Susan B. Anthony dedicated her life to fighting for women's right to vote. In the process, she led a revolution without bloodshed.

Sometimes you have to fight softly.
And sometimes you have to fight loudly.
Susan B. Anthony fought loudly.

In 1872, she went to vote in the presidential election.
The poll workers refused.
They said she couldn't vote. Because she was a woman.
Back then, in America—and around the world—women didn't have that right.

But when she started quoting the 14th Amendment and its recognition that *all* citizens—
not just men—were entitled to rights, she convinced the poll workers they had no choice.
She cast her vote—and was later arrested for it. For breaking the law.

At the trial, all her logical arguments didn't matter.
The judge apparently wrote his decision before even hearing the case.
He then instructed the jury to find her guilty and fined her one hundred dollars.

Susan B. Anthony told the judge she'd never pay. Never.

She never did.
And though the judge thought he got the last laugh by refusing to imprison her,
therefore denying her an appeal to the U.S. Supreme Court,
Susan B. Anthony made three thousand copies of the trial proceedings and sent them to
activists and politicians across the country, making sure they all heard her voice.

In 1877, she gathered ten thousand signatures on petitions from twenty-six states.
Congress still didn't care.
For over thirty years, she appeared before every Congress, asking for a new amendment
that would give the vote to women.
They always said no.

When she died in 1906, women still didn't have the right to vote.
That didn't come until 1920. But was she heard?
When the Nineteenth Amendment was finally passed, it was also known as the *Susan B.
Anthony Amendment.*

Failure is impossible. —SUSAN B. ANTHONY's final public words

NANCY G. BRINKER

Founder of Susan G. Komen for the Cure.

Nancy Brinker has built one of the leading organizations of the breast cancer movement. Today, more than a million people run in the Susan G. Komen Race for the Cure, raising almost $2 billion over the past quarter century.

I lost my mother to breast cancer.

You lost your Nana.

And your great-grandmother Sara, whom you're named after.

In 1980, Nancy Brinker lost her sister.

As her sister was dying, she said, "Promise me, Nanny. Promise me you won't let it go on like this."

Her heart broken, Nancy promised: "I swear, Suzy. Even if it takes the rest of my life."

In 1982, with two hundred dollars and a shoe box containing the names of friends, Nancy started her own organization. She named it in honor of her sister: Susan G. Komen.
Back then, pink ribbons had nothing to do with breast cancer. Today, they're the heart of one of the most successful awareness campaigns in history.
Back then, the government spent barely $30 million on research. Today, it spends $900 million.
Back then, the five-year survival rate, when cancer was caught before it spread beyond the breast, was 74 percent. Today, thanks to the work of millions of people, it's as high as 98 percent.

That's close. But not enough.

For my mother . . . for your Nana . . . for every woman out there . . .

The battle must continue.

In the months after making that promise, Nancy lay awake at night wondering if one person can really make a difference. Nancy's life is the answer.

—PRESIDENT BARACK OBAMA

CLARA BARTON

Schoolteacher. Activist.
Founder of the American Red Cross.

Before the Civil War, Clara Barton was a shy schoolteacher who brought public education to New Jersey. But her greatest gift was when she brought the Red Cross to America.

During the Civil War, when the new U.S. Capitol building served as an impromptu
hospital, she was there to help the injured.

First she organized relief in the form of clothing, food, and simple utensils.
Then she went a step further by venturing onto the battlefield,
carrying crackers, coffee, and medical supplies.
She brought more than aid to the soldiers—she brought comfort.

When a sergeant had his arms destroyed by a shell burst, she was the one who made sure
he'd have an attendant to help him . . . and full pay until his pension came.

When a bullet ripped through the sleeve of her dress and killed
the soldier whom she had bent down to give a drink,
Clara didn't turn around.
She didn't run away.
She bravely kept working, despite the dangers.

When the surgeons could no longer operate after sunset, Clara presented them with
lanterns, and just like her, they kept working, too.

It was acts like these that made a difference to one soldier, and then another.
It *is* acts like these that enable the Red Cross to help so many.
And it all began with one woman who refused to turn away.

*It irritates me to be told how things always have been done. . . . I cannot afford the luxury of
a closed mind. I go for anything new that might improve the past.*   —CLARA BARTON

*At a time when we were entirely out of dressings of every kind, she supplied us with
everything, and while the shells were bursting in every direction . . . she staid [sic] dealing
out shirts . . . and preparing soup. . . . I thought that night that if heaven ever sent out a
homely angel, she must be one.*
                    —UNION ARMY SURGEON DR. JAMES I. DUNN, in a letter to his wife

SHEILA SPICER

Teacher.

As my ninth-grade English teacher, Sheila Spicer was the first person to ever tell me I was good at writing.

When I was fifteen, my ninth-grade English teacher told me I was in the wrong class.

"You can write," she said.

From there, Ms. Spicer tried to move me to the honors class, but because of a conflict in my schedule, it wouldn't work.

So she took me aside and told me:

"For this entire year, I want you to ignore everything I do at the blackboard. Ignore all the homework assignments I give. Ignore all the discussions. Instead, you're going to sit here and do the honors work."

And I did.

What she was really saying was: *You'll thank me later.*

A decade passed, and when my first novel was published, I went back to Ms. Spicer's class and knocked on the door.

"Can I help you?" she asked. (Of course she didn't recognize me; the last time she saw me, I had a full head of hair.)

"My name is Brad Meltzer," I told her, handing her a copy of my first book. "And I wrote this book for *you.*"

Within seconds, she was crying.

When I asked her *why*, she told me she was thinking about retiring because she didn't feel she was having an impact anymore.

"Are you kidding?" I asked. "You have thirty students. We have only *one* teacher."

When I was fifteen, Sheila Spicer changed my life.

So as you get older, I want you to remember the first person who tells you you're good at something.

And thank them.

> *"Do not give up on these kids!"*
> —SHEILA SPICER, to a roomful of teachers at her retirement party—
> in 2010, more than thirteen years after she first *threatened to retire*

WINSTON CHURCHILL

Prime minister of Great Britain.

With unblinking intensity and stirring wartime oratories, Winston Churchill inspired both Great Britain and the Allied powers, leading the charge to victory against the Axis powers in World War II.

In 1940, during World War II, England was being pummeled by aerial assaults—and worse, they were all alone.

The United States wasn't officially involved yet.

France had already fallen.

So as the Battle of Britain approached,

as the blitz was ready to rain bombs from the sky—and the people of London would run to sleep in subway stations—

it was a time when England's spirit should've been broken.

Instead, Prime Minister Winston Churchill took to the airwaves.

He told all of Great Britain, "If we fail, then the whole world, including the United States, including all that we have known and cared for, will sink into the abyss. . . ."

He told them that "whatever the cost may be, we shall fight on the beaches, we shall fight on the landing grounds, we shall fight in the fields and in the streets, we shall fight in the hills; we shall never surrender. . . ."

He told them this would be "their finest hour."

And it was.

Just as it was his.

Today, I can tell you the moral of the story—

but it was Churchill, as usual, who said it best:

"Never give in. Never give in. Never, never, never, never—in nothing, great or small, large or petty—never give in, except to convictions of honor and good sense."

You have enemies? Good. That means you've stood up for something, sometime in your life.
—WINSTON CHURCHILL

LISA SIMPSON

Sax player. Middle child.

Being part of the most famous cartoon family in history, Lisa Simpson proves that having brains is the coolest thing of all.

She wanted the doll so badly—the special "Talking" Malibu Stacy doll.
But when she finally heard the doll speak, Lisa was heartbroken.
Much like the real-life Barbie doll that said, "Math class is tough," Malibu Stacy said:
"I wish they taught shopping in school,"
"Thinking too much gives you wrinkles,"
and "Don't ask me, I'm just a girl," quickly followed by a giggle.

Lisa could've just ignored the doll.
Instead, she took action—and made her own doll: "Lisa Lionheart."
Its catchphrase?
"Trust in yourself, and you can achieve anything."

Did the "Lisa Lionheart" doll sell?
Not at all.
Malibu Stacy was still on top.

I don't care.

There's a reason Lisa's the smartest member of her family.
She knows that when you see something you think is wrong,
that's *always* when you need to take action.

If cartoons were meant for adults, they'd put them on in prime time. —LISA SIMPSON

ELEANOR ROOSEVELT

Activist. Role model. Wife of President Franklin Delano Roosevelt.

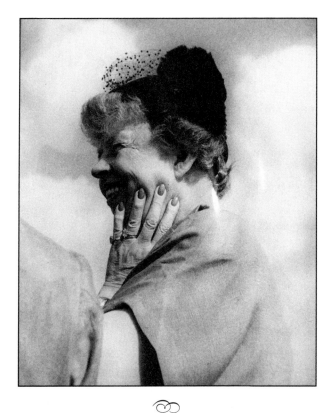

The first lady during the Great Depression and World War II, Eleanor Roosevelt became a fighter for women's rights, minorities' rights, and social justice.

In 1932, seventeen thousand veterans and their families descended on Washington D.C. and built a tent city, demanding what they believed were overdue payments for their service during World War I.

President Hoover sent General Douglas MacArthur and troops armed with fixed bayonets to meet the veterans with force. With tanks. With tear gas.

By March 1933, when the veterans returned, FDR was president. Instead of sending the army, he sent his wife, Eleanor Roosevelt.

The first lady went to the tent city. Alone.

In mud and rain, she walked among the veterans. She talked to them like people. She listened.

Soon after, an executive order was issued that created twenty-five thousand jobs for veterans through the Civilian Conservation Corps and eventually led to the 1944 passage of the GI Bill of Rights, which gave veterans federal assistance in returning to civilian life.

No one can make you feel inferior without your consent. —ELEANOR ROOSEVELT

Many journalists suggested that if Eleanor Roosevelt wanted to comment on politics, she should do it off the record. That wasn't her way.

"I am making these statements on purpose," she said, "to arouse controversy and thereby get the topics talked about."

Race relations, the suffrage movement, poverty—every topic was fair game. Indeed, President Roosevelt didn't publicly support civil rights for black people—until after the first lady started speaking out against the social injustice of Jim Crow laws.

TINA TURNER

Singer. Rock 'n' Roll legend.

Named one of the 100 Greatest Artists of All Time by *Rolling Stone*, Tina Turner is a true rock 'n' roll icon. For more than fifty years, her powerful vocals and even more powerful energy have made her one of the world's most popular entertainers.

For sixteen years, her husband beat her.

But on this night, Tina Turner washed the blood from her face, wrapped a cape around her bloodied clothes, covered her eyes with a pair of sunglasses, and placed a wrap on her head, because the swelling was so bad, she couldn't wear her wig.

She ran out of the hotel, hid among the trash cans, and then ran to the Ramada Inn, where she begged for a room.

All she had was thirty-six cents and a Mobil credit card.

But after sixteen years of cruelty, she finally walked out on Ike Turner.

To be clear, it wasn't easy. She was so worried about her safety, she stayed with friends, paying her way by keeping house. It got so bad that Tina Turner—*the* Tina Turner—had to use food stamps.

And yes, it's incredible that Tina Turner built her career back from nothing.

But what's even more incredible is the battle cry she repeated inside her head—the battle cry that gave her strength: "I will die before I go back."

Never forget it: No matter how deep the hole is, you can always find a way out.

In their divorce, Tina Turner gave Ike nearly everything. All their money. And the publishing royalties for her compositions. "You take everything I've made in the last sixteen years," she said. "I'll take my future."

THE THREE STOOGES

Slapstick comedians.

Comedy geniuses who paraded as fools, Moe, Curly, and Larry made audiences laugh for decades with their slapstick short films. Plus, they had a weapon no one could fight: humor.

I know.

You're laughing, right?

But back during World War II, at a time when Hollywood—and the rest of the country—were still hesitant about confronting Nazi Germany, it was these three who were the brave ones.

Why?

Because on January 19, 1940—nearly two years before Pearl Harbor—it was the Three Stooges who took on Adolf Hitler.

Sure, Charlie Chaplin got the credit for ridiculing Hitler in *The Great Dictator*. But it was actually Moe Howard who was the first film actor to make fun of Hitler onscreen.

The Three Stooges film *You Nazty Spy!* beat Chaplin by a full nine months, ripping the German dictator for book burnings, the infamous appeasement at Munich, and even for a "concentrated camp."

At the time, America's official position was neutrality. Hollywood was under great pressure to remain isolationist and avoid propaganda. Despite that, the Stooges—all of them Jewish—took their shot.

By doing so, they inspired and emboldened others to do exactly the same.

And that, without question, is nothing to laugh at.

Our genius ain't appreciated around here . . . let's scram!"
—MOE, in *Movie Maniacs*, 1936

You Nazty Spy! *was Moe Howard's favorite Stooges film.*

WANGARI MAATHAI

Founder of the Green Belt Movement.
First African woman to win the Nobel Prize.

To respond to the needs of rural women in Kenya, Wangari Maathai began with a simple idea: plant a tree. What grew from there was more than anyone expected.

It started with seven trees.
That's all she planted at first. Just seven.

Yes, it was a way to fight deforestation and soil erosion.
And yes, it helped create jobs for women and launch the Green Belt Movement.

But the reason Wangari Maathai physically and politically changed the landscape of Kenya
is because, when she planted those first seven trees,
she believed in an individual's—a woman's—power to change this world for the better.

For that reason, the Kenyan government called her movement "subversive."
The Kenyan President called her "mad" and a "threat to the order and security of the country."
And her husband divorced her for being "too educated" and hard to control.

But here's why she couldn't be stopped:
Her idea was now out there.
They arrested her and beat her unconscious for protesting.
But women kept planting trees. Little acts of change that added up.
In 1999, when she planted trees to protest the destruction of a forest for luxury homes, the security guards whipped and clubbed her.
Refusing to be silenced, Maathai demanded to sign the police report *in her own blood*.

Women kept planting trees. And kept planting trees.
What started as seven trees reached over thirty million.

In 2004, Maathai became the first African woman to receive the Nobel Peace Prize.
Upon hearing of her honor, she celebrated . . .
by planting a tree.
"That's the way I do things when I want to celebrate. I always plant a tree."

It's the little things citizens do. That's what will make the difference. My little thing is
planting trees.   —WANGARI MAATHAI

AGATHA CHRISTIE

Queen of crime.

Agatha Christie is one of the most popular and successful mystery writers in history. According to her publisher, her stories of crime and murder are outsold only by the Bible and Shakespeare.

Stories aren't the beauty of what *did happen*.
They're the beauty of what *could happen*.

For that reason, you'll never forget when you read a great book.

And that's why I'll never forget this woman.

When I was ten, I picked up her novel *Murder at the Vicarage*.
It was the first murder mystery I'd ever read.
To this day, I still don't know what a vicarage is. And I don't want to.
Back then, all I cared about was that on those pages . . . there was a body.
A *dead body*.

How'd it get there?
Why'd it happen?
And the most vital question of all: Whodunit?

I've been asking that question ever since.
It was the first great book I remember reading.
But Agatha Christie isn't amazing because she influenced me to be a mystery writer . . .
She's amazing because she's *proof* of how a well-told story can change someone's life.

The young people think the old people are fools—but the old people know the young people
are fools.
                                        —AGATHA CHRISTIE, *Murder at the Vicarage*

LEONARDO DA VINCI

Artist. Engineer. Painter. Architect. Sculptor. Inventor.

Although most people know him as the painter of the *Mona Lisa* and *The Last Supper*, Italian genius Leonardo da Vinci challenged the world in nearly every category of thinking.

The tank.
The submarine.
The helicopter.
A hang glider.
Scuba equipment.
Wings, based on bats, that would let him fly.

Leonardo da Vinci dreamed them all up years before anyone else.
Almost five hundred years, to be exact.

And every single one of them failed.

The wings didn't help him fly.
The scuba gear was made from a suit of leather.
His pre-helicopter never took off.

But.
Over time, as technology and human innovation caught up with his ideas . . .
Every single one of them *worked*.

Remember it always:
Be daring.
Be daring.
Always be daring.
There is no big dream unless you dream big.

> *Anyone who conducts an argument by appealing to authority is not using his intelligence; he is just using his memory.*   —LEONARDO DA VINCI

DOLLY PARTON

Legendary singer-songwriter.
Businesswoman.

With 25 number-one singles, 41 top-ten country albums, 7 Grammys—
including a lifetime achievement award—plus one of the world's most successful
theme parks, Dolly Parton isn't just a respected singer-songwriter. She's
responsible for the growth of country music throughout the world.

The fourth of twelve children, Dolly Parton grew up in a one-room cabin in the foothills of the Great Smoky Mountains.

She didn't have electricity. Or running water.

But she had family—and she had faith—and that's all she needed to find her music.

At five, she wrote her first song.

At seven, she *made* her first guitar by putting two bass guitar strings on a mandolin.

And the day after high school graduation, she moved to Nashville.

Today, she's written more than three thousand songs.

But that's not why people love her. They love her because *despite* her fame and talents, she never forgot her roots.

Want proof?

To "inspire children in her home community to dream more, learn more, care more and be more," Dolly Parton began the Imagination Library.

Each month, children under five were mailed a new book to teach them the value of reading.

The first book was always *The Little Engine That Could*.

Today, like the little engine, Dolly Parton can go anywhere.

But to keep herself grounded—when she wants to write or just center herself—she still goes to the Smoky Mountain foothills . . . to the exact spot where the one-room shack used to sit.

She could've built a mansion there. Instead, she rebuilt the little cabin.

Just like the one from her childhood.

Some people never change—and believe it or not, that's a good thing.

The way I see it, if you want the rainbow, you gotta put up with the rain.

—DOLLY PARTON

After starting in Tennessee, the Imagination Library is now in more than 1,300 communities.

SOJOURNER TRUTH

Abolitionist. Speaker. Fighter.

Born into slavery and beaten by her owners, Sojourner Truth channeled her experiences and became one of America's most outspoken campaigners for women's rights and racial equality.

In 1827, when she heard that her five-year-old son had illegally been sold back into slavery, Isabella walked to the home of her former mistress—the woman who had abused her so cruelly—and confronted her.

The mistress couldn't believe the "fuss" Isabella was making.

But Isabella promised her: "I'll have my child again."

The former slave had no idea how a courthouse worked.

She went up to a man who looked "grand," since she was told to find the grand jury.

As she swore upon the Bible, the clerks laughed, one of them asking what good it would be to have her swear upon a Bible.

But she never stopped. Her complaint was filed.

And eventually, she won.

Her son was returned. Completely free.

At that moment, she could've rested. The fight for her son's freedom was over.

But she knew: there was so much more to fight for.

Changing her name to "Sojourner Truth," she spoke across the country, fighting for gender and racial equality.

She fought her way to the White House, where she met with Abraham Lincoln.

She even fought against the fact that streetcars were segregated by race—ninety years before Rosa Parks sat down in the front of that bus.

Sometimes she won. Often, Sojourner Truth lost.

But she fought. She always fought.

As I hope you always do.

I will shake every place I go to. —SOJOURNER TRUTH

Sojourner Truth never learned to read or write. She dictated everything she wrote, including her life story.

BRANCH RICKEY

General manager of the Brooklyn Dodgers.

Years before the military or public schools were integrated, Branch Rickey made civil rights—and baseball—history by signing Jackie Robinson to the Brooklyn Dodgers.

In 1903, the Ohio Wesleyan University baseball team arrived at the hotel where they were supposed to stay before the next day's game.

But when a hotel employee saw that one of the players was black, he told twenty-one-year-old head coach Branch Rickey that the black player couldn't stay there—the hotel was for whites only.

After talking with the hotel manager, Rickey eventually convinced the hotel to allow the black player to stay in Coach Rickey's room, on a cot.

Once in the room, the black player broke down, sobbing.
He began vigorously rubbing at his own hands, saying, "Black skin . . . black skin. If I only could rub it off and make 'em white."

"I never felt so helpless in my life," Branch Rickey later said.

Forty years later, the young white coach was now the president and general manager of the Brooklyn Dodgers. In all of major-league baseball, not a single team had even one black player.

With many major leaguers fighting in World War II, Rickey went to the league board of directors with a plan to scout new players.
He added this twist: the Dodgers would also, secretly, scout blacks.
In Rickey's eyes, it was time to integrate baseball.

"Why should you be the one to do it?" his wife pleaded. "Haven't you done enough for baseball? Can't someone else do something for a change?"
And the truth is, she was right. Someone else could have.
But no one did.

In 1945, never forgetting that night at the hotel, Branch Rickey broke baseball's color barrier by inviting a young man named Jackie Robinson to be the first black player in the all-white league.

It's one thing to recognize injustice when you see it.
It's quite another to do something about it.

The thing about him was that he was always doing something for someone else. I know, because he did so much for me.
—JACKIE ROBINSON

LUCILLE BALL

Actor. Trailblazer.

The star and creative force behind the early TV show *I Love Lucy*, Lucille Ball became the greatest comedian of her time and one of the most beloved entertainers ever—solely through her ability to find a laugh in what everyone else was taking so seriously.

She was sent to live with Grandmother Peterson.
Grandmother Peterson believed happiness was a sin.

In her house, mirrors were banned—except the one in the bathroom—since they led to vanity.

Instead, Lucy would play in the chicken coop, pretending it was her castle, the chickens her loyal army.
For friends? Lucy created one: "Sassafrassa."

Only Sassafrassa gave Lucy compliments, telling Lucy she was far more beautiful than Grandmother knew.
Lucy needed to hear it. If she was caught looking in the mirror, she was punished.

This was the girl who relished the chance to see her own reflection.
Contorting her face and widening her eyes in trolley car windows, she loved to see the possibilities. The simple humor of it.

And as she proved to the world, that humor could take on anything.

"Love yourself first and everything falls into line." —LUCILLE BALL

Between 1952 and 1953, when TV studio executives thought no one would watch the wacky redhead and her Cuban husband, on a typical Monday night two out of three households with TV sets proved them wrong.

ELIZABETH BLACKBURN

Nobel Prize winner.

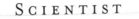

Biologist Elizabeth Blackburn won the Nobel Prize for discovering the enzyme telomerase, which protects the integrity of genes and stabilizes chromosomes. Her research is now being used to understand aging and to decipher some of the world's greatest diseases.

Do you know what "convention" is?
Convention is a belief that's shared by so many people, it starts to be become a custom.

But know one thing:
"Convention" is very different from "truth."

So.
The convention used to be that girls weren't as good at science, technology, engineering, or math.
That is wrong.
Study after study shows that girls perform just as well as boys in all those fields.
So where did the problem start? Girls were told they weren't capable, and people wrongly believed it.

As a child, Elizabeth Blackburn was told the opposite.
Her parents always encouraged her love of science.
When she used to draw pictures of amino acids and hang them in her room, they never took them down.
When she asked for a microscope for Christmas, they bought her one, never telling her, "Girls don't want microscopes."

So as your parent, let me tell you: There are no limits. There are no boundaries.

In the end, Dr. Blackburn won the Nobel Prize for her efforts studying, among other things, chromosomes.
But what's far more important is that chromosomes—whether they make you man or woman—never limit what you're capable of.

I believed then and still do that I loved science because it also became a world in which I could escape, in the way that for some people religion is an escape into a world where things are fair and you know where you stand. I remember being able to articulate clearly in my mind at quite a young age . . . that through science I could escape into a world where things were secure and fair.
—ELIZABETH BLACKBURN

ELLA FITZGERALD

Jazz singer. Music icon.

With her soulful voice and up-tempo melodies, the "First Lady of Song," Ella Fitzgerald, defined an age of American jazz and pop music.

Sometimes you're given a moment.

Back when Ella was at a New York state reform school, she'd been held in the basement and nearly tortured.

At age fifteen, she was scrounging for money, trying to survive during the Great Depression.

But at the age of seventeen, she won the chance via lottery to perform at an amateur contest held by the Apollo Theater.

This was her moment—and she wasn't going to sing.

She came to dance. Her routine was set . . .

Until she saw that the main show's closing act was the Edwards Sisters—a hot duo who Ella thought were "the dancingest sisters around."

Ella couldn't follow that.

At that moment on the stage, she panicked.

The crowd started to boo at the plain and unkempt girl.

She could have withered right there, and we might've never heard her name, let alone her voice.

But at that moment, Ella Fitzgerald didn't leave. Instead, she made the decision to sing the old song that her mother loved called "Judy."

And there it was. The girl with the voice of a cheering trumpet.

When she was done, they wanted an encore. So Ella kept singing.

She won Amateur Night. Twenty-five dollars.

Sometimes you're given a moment.

What matters is what you do with it.

The only thing better than singing is more singing.—ELLA FITZGERALD

MAHATMA GANDHI

Spiritual leader. Political icon. Pacifist.

Through nonviolent civil disobedience, political and spiritual leader Mohandas
Gandhi united India in a struggle for independence. Known as Mahatma—
"The Great Soul"—he fought for religious tolerance, economic self-sufficiency,
and the end of British rule over his country. He went to prison. He fasted. He
preached. But Gandhi never raised his hand in anger. It worked.

One day, you will fight.

So how should you fight?

With your fists? With threats? With words? With weapons?

They all work. They've been tested—successfully—for centuries.

But to fight by purposely avoiding violence?

To refuse to raise your fist, no matter what is raised against you?

Some would call that *lunacy*.

Madness.

But what it really is, is *courage*.

In a gentle way, you can shake the world. —MAHATMA GANDHI

Whenever you are confronted with an opponent, conquer him with love.
—MAHATMA GANDHI

MARY SHELLEY

Author of Frankenstein.

Published nearly two hundred years ago, *Frankenstein* by Mary Shelley is still one of the greatest horror tales of all time.

Think about science fiction. Think about the robots and the space voyages and the mad scientists. Got it?

Good.

Now think about the person who ushered in the age of modern science fiction.
You should be picturing an eighteen-year-old girl, who gathered around a fireplace with friends to read ghost stories.
One of those friends, Lord Byron, proposed they each try their hand at crafting a ghostly tale.

Almost immediately, the three men began forming ideas.
The famed poets Percy Shelley and Lord Byron began thinking of theirs.
Young Mary had nothing. How could this girl compare to these great, poetic men?
But Mary kept pressing herself, refusing to give up on it, even after the men had cast their stories aside.

It finally came to her as she lay in bed—the idea for the novel she would finish at age nineteen:
And that's how *Frankenstein* was born,
along with modern science fiction.

That's right—all from a teenage girl who kept pushing herself.
Her creation will never die.

> *There is something at work in my soul which I do not understand. I am practically industrious—painstaking; a workman to execute with perseverance and labour:—but besides this, there is a love for the marvellous, a belief in the marvellous, intertwined in all my projects, which hurries me out of the common pathways of men, even to the wild sea and unvisited regions I am about to explore.*
> —MARY SHELLEY, *Frankenstein*

ROCHELLE SHORETZ

Lawyer. Advocate. Survivor.

Rochelle Shoretz is the first Orthodox woman law clerk to serve at the U.S. Supreme Court, and the first woman to serve while raising two small children. She is also the founder and executive director of Sharsheret (Hebrew for "chain"), an organization dedicated to addressing the challenges of young Jewish women and their families with breast cancer. In this photo, she's doing the New York City triathlon with Stage Four breast cancer.

It's not because she was a Supreme Court clerk to Justice Ruth Bader Ginsburg.

It's not because, when she was diagnosed with breast cancer at the young age of twenty-eight, she refused to give up.

And it's not even because, when she found that there weren't any breast cancer organizations that dealt with the particular issues facing young Jewish women, she started her own national organization, Sharsheret, which has since educated and comforted thousands of young women suffering from the disease.

It's simply because, when her own cancer came back, my law school friend Rochelle Shoretz never lost her enthusiasm, her spark, or her priceless sense of humor.

"How you doing?" I would ask.
"Except for dying from breast cancer, I'm great," she'd reply with a smile.

Ten years after her diagnosis, she's still doing great.

Strong. Fearless. And always herself.
That's what great women are made of.

You have to laugh! Life is too short. —ROCHELLE SHORETZ

TANK MAN

Tiananmen Square protester.

As pro-democracy students protested in Beijing's Tiananmen Square, the Chinese government unleashed its military. One protester stood up for what he believed in by standing in its way.

The Chinese soldiers had shot people in their backs.

When an ambulance drove to the scene to help the injured, the medics were killed too. There was no mercy, just violence.

And on June 5, 1989, the government had won. The student protest was over. Tyranny had conquered peace.

Until one man made a literal stand.

As a line of tanks crawled into Tiananmen Square, a lone man in a white shirt and black pants walked onto the street and blocked the lead tank.

Instead of running the man over, the tank turned right to go around him. But the lone man, carrying only shopping bags, quickly moved to his left and again cut off the tank.

When the tank again shifted, the man moved with it, like a defiant dance partner.

His message was clear: He wouldn't back down. He'd stand in their way.

And the whole world saw it.

To this day, no one knows his name. No one knows who he is.

But his lesson will never be forgotten: Bullies can suppress us. But they can never stop us.

What this young man did was, in effect, change the world.
—BRUCE HERSCHENSOHN, Pepperdine University

BILLIE JEAN KING

Tennis legend. Giant slayer.

Tennis player Billie Jean King won thirty-nine Grand Slam titles and has been a champion of women's athletics on and off the tennis court.

Former tennis star Bobby Riggs said that no female tennis player could beat him. That women weren't as good as men.

So in 1973, Margaret Court, a top-ranked female tennis star, took him on.
She lost.
Learning of Court's loss from a radio report, feminist and tennis star Billie Jean King called her husband and said, "Larry, now we've got something to prove."

Bobby Riggs taunted her. Said that Billie Jean King could never win.
She didn't care. She took him on.
And in three straight sets, in front of 90 million viewers, she beat him. Devastated him. Easily.

Looking back, it seems so obvious.
Of course a twenty-nine-year-old athlete can take down a fifty-five-year-old loudmouth.
But back then, all the experts—and the Vegas odds, and even fellow female tennis players—said the man would win. Simply because he was a man.

Indeed, in 1973, the only thing that *was* obvious was that talent didn't matter when gender was involved.
And *that's* why this game mattered, my daughter.

Sometimes, a bias is just so ingrained, the only way to change perception is to show people the truth.

In three sets, Billie Jean King didn't just break a glass ceiling.
She used a small felt ball to smash an idea.

Billie Jean King is one of the all-time tennis greats, she's one of the superstars, she's ready for the big one, but she doesn't stand a chance against me....
—BOBBY RIGGS, before losing to Billie Jean King

THE HEROES OF UNITED FLIGHT 93

Lifesavers.

On September 11, 2001, after terrorists attacked New York City and Washington, D.C., a group of passengers on United Flight 93 courageously fought to take control of their aircraft—and destiny—by refusing to let their plane be used as another weapon.

We owe these forty men and women.

We owe them personally.

"They're talking about crashing this plane into the ground. We have to do something," Thomas Burnett Jr. told his wife, Deena, on his cell phone. "I'm putting a plan together."

"Who's helping you?" his wife asked.

"Different people. Several people. There's a group of us. Don't worry. I'll call you back," he replied.

Flight attendant Sandra Bradshaw called her husband and said that she was boiling water as a weapon. Her final words: "Everyone's running to first class. I've got to go. Bye."

"Let's roll," Todd Beamer famously added as they rushed to the front of the plane, likely using a beverage cart as a battering ram to break into the locked cockpit.

Thanks to their bravery, their Boeing 757 crashed in a field in Shanksville, Pennsylvania, never reaching the terrorists' real target.
It was approximately twenty minutes from Washington, D.C., where the plane would've struck either the White House or, more likely, the U.S. Capitol.

That's right.

The U.S. Capitol—where your mother worked.
That morning, on September 11, 2001, she was eight months pregnant and was driving to work at the Capitol.

Every passenger—and all the terrorists—lost their lives in the crash.
But their bravery saved so many others.

We will owe these men and women forever.

Don't worry, we're going to do something.
—THOMAS BURNETT JR., on the phone with his wife, Deena

TEMPLE GRANDIN

Autism activist. Role model.

Rather than view her autism spectrum diagnosis as a detriment, Dr. Temple Grandin used her unique perspective to prove it was her greatest strength.

Temple Grandin didn't speak until she was nearly four.
As someone on the autistic spectrum, she could only scream and groan.
Her doctors said she should be put in an institution.
Her mother refused, determined to let her experience the world.

Lucky for us, that's exactly what Grandin did.

You see, Temple Grandin's brain doesn't work like yours or mine.
She thinks "in pictures."
If someone says the word *factory*, most of us think of a generic place.
She sees the details—the tiny details—of specific factories she's seen.
As a result, she sees what we can't.

She used that skill on a farm as she watched the cruelty of the slaughterhouse. When she stepped into the cow's chutes, she understood their point of view, noticing details that everyone else missed.
Because of her ability to think in pictures—not despite it, but *because of it*—she revolutionized the cattle industry.
Indeed, her "disorder" was what made her great.

She still has her difficulties, like coping with loud noises and the "itch" of pants.
But until Temple Grandin told her story, many professionals and parents saw an autism diagnosis as a guarantee that their child wouldn't have a fulfilling life.

Today, we know that greatness rests in every mind.

The world needs all kinds of minds. —TEMPLE GRANDIN

If I could snap my fingers and become nonautistic I would not—because then I wouldn't be me. Autism is part of who I am.
　　　　　　　　　　　　　　　　　　　　　　　—TEMPLE GRANDIN

One out of every 110 children in the United States has an autism spectrum disorder.

ROSA PARKS

Mother of the civil rights movement.

On a crowded bus in 1955, African American seamstress Rosa Parks refused to give up her seat to a white man. Her act of defiance ignited the Montgomery Bus Boycott, which lasted 381 days. Then public busing segregation came to an end. And a movement began.

Yes, she was tired.

She had grown up with the Ku Klux Klan riding past her house, her grandfather standing guard with the shotgun.

She had endured seeing her school burn down—twice.

She had faced this bus driver before, when he left her to walk five miles in the rain because she sat down in the white section to pick up her purse.

She had lived with injustice her entire life.

Yes, she was tired.

But it wasn't the kind of *tired* that came from aching feet.

"The only tired I was was tired of giving in."

So when the bus driver motioned to her to stand and give her seat away to a white person, the seamstress from Montgomery, Alabama, refused.

"Well, I'm going to have you arrested," the bus driver said.

Rosa Parks calmly replied, "You may go on and do so."

For violating Chapter 6, Section 11, of the Montgomery City Code, Rosa Parks went to jail.

For standing up for herself—by sitting down—Rosa Parks ignited a movement.

All I was doing was trying to get home from work. —ROSA PARKS

JANE GOODALL

Famed primatologist. Environmental advocate.

Armed with little more than a notebook and a pair of binoculars, Jane Goodall immersed herself in the jungles of Tanzania to begin an unprecedented career of studying chimpanzees. Her findings have redefined the animal kingdom.

In the summer of 1960, she arrived in what is now Tanzania.
The chimpanzees that she was studying would run whenever she came into sight.
Using binoculars, she inched closer. The animals slowly got used to her.

Soon, she started naming the chimps.
She wasn't supposed to. Animals were supposed to get numbers, not names.
Why?
So scientists wouldn't project human attributes on the animals.

But in Goodall's eyes, only by looking at the chimps as individuals could she truly understand them.

It made all the difference.

As she watched, two of the chimps—one named David Greybeard, the other named Goliath—began stripping leaves from twigs and sticking them down the mound of a termite hole.
Goodall saw it. She realized that they weren't just using tools.
They were *making* them.
No doubt, these animals were intelligent.

Over time, she learned that the animals had their own personalities and complex personal relationships.

By following her gut instead of following the rules, Jane Goodall didn't just change how we look at animal intelligence.

She changed how we look at the world.

You cannot get through a single day without having an impact on the world around you. What you do makes a difference, and you have to decide what kind of difference you want to make.
—JANE GOODALL

THE DALAI LAMA

World leader. Buddhist monk.

The Dalai Lama was awarded the Nobel Peace Prize for his unwavering commitment to nonviolence while seeking to establish an independent Tibetan state. To this day, he describes himself only as a simple Buddhist monk.

In 1959, the Buddhist leader known as the Dalai Lama was forced to flee his home in Tibet.

He had every reason to be bitter and enraged:
His enemies had driven him out.
They stopped him from returning home.
And, as in any heated argument, both sides were claiming the other was being unreasonable.

So what was the Dalai Lama's reaction?

He's spent the past fifty years trying to spread a message of love and understanding.

According to the small smiling monk, life's real purpose is to find happiness.
He says the secret to happiness comes from developing love and compassion for all people.
For your family.
For your friends.
Even for your enemies.

No question, it's a lesson that's easier said than done.

But whatever side you're on—whether you're arguing about religion, politics, or anything else—it is a message worth sharing.

Remember that not getting what you want is sometimes a wonderful stroke of luck.
—THE DALAI LAMA

ABRAHAM LINCOLN

Lawyer. Speaker. President.

One of America's greatest leaders, Abraham Lincoln lost eight elections. Despite those defeats, he became the sixteenth president of the United States and held the country together during the bloodshed of the Civil War.

Today there is a phrase for it: political suicide.

It's what happens when you say something that most people disagree with.

In 1858, while Abraham Lincoln was trying to get elected in Illinois to the United States Senate, his rival, Stephen Douglas, represented "most people."

Douglas said that blacks had no rights.

He said that the promise of life, liberty, and the pursuit of happiness did not apply to them.

The Supreme Court of the United States agreed.

But Abraham Lincoln didn't.

Lincoln stood up.

Lincoln spoke his mind.

And Lincoln lost.

He was sent home with nothing.

It *was* political suicide.

But it was worth it.

I am not bound to win, but I am bound to be true. I am not bound to succeed, but I am bound to live by the light that I have. I must stand with anybody that stands right, and stand with him while he is right, and part with him when he goes wrong. —ABRAHAM LINCOLN

THURGOOD MARSHALL

First black U. S. Supreme Court justice.

A legendary lawyer, Thurgood Marshall made his name arguing some of the greatest cases of the civil rights movement, including *Brown v. Board of Education*. As a Supreme Court Justice, he spent decades fighting for the disenfranchised.

While researching this book for you, I was lucky enough to talk to Thurgood Marshall's son.

I asked him about his father and all that he'd achieved.
I asked him about what kind of person he was.
I asked what he remembered most about him.
But what I really wanted to know was "How?"

How did he get there?

How did Thurgood Marshall manage to take one of the world's most important cases to the Supreme Court—and win?

I was hoping Marshall's son would reveal some great secret. And he did.

He told me that everyone always remembers his father's biggest case, *Brown v. Board of Education*.
They remember how it ended school segregation and paved the way for the civil rights movement.
But he explained, his father tried thirty-two cases before the Supreme Court.
And you don't get the big case until you do all the ones that come before.

For a moment, I sat there, kicking myself for missing the obvious.

How did Thurgood Marshall get his big chance?
The same way I hope you get yours.
You earn it.

The legal system can force open doors, and sometimes even knock down walls. But it cannot build bridges. That job belongs to you and me.
　　　　　　　　　　　　　　　　　　　—THURGOOD MARSHALL

DOROTHEA LANGE

Photographer.

Through the photographs she took, Dorothea Lange gave a human face to the poor, the hungry, and the unemployed during the Great Depression.

In her early unforgettable photographic work, she took pictures of people standing on breadlines during the Great Depression.

From there, the Franklin Roosevelt administration took notice and asked Dorothea Lange to take photos of struggling migrant workers.

The result was *Migrant Mother*, the photograph on the opposite page of thirty-two-year-old Florence Owens Thompson, whose husband and seven children were sheltered at a pea picker's camp.
The picture gave the Depression a face that would never be forgotten.

In 1942, the government again approached Lange, asking her to document the internment of Japanese Americans. They didn't plan to close the camps, only to record them.
The more than eight hundred photos she took showed the truth about the camps: that our own government evacuated people from their homes and forced them to live in horse stalls and bare shacks.
When the government saw the results, they impounded the photos.

It's because they knew what Dorothea Lange's true power was.

Her photos didn't just tell stories.
They made us see the truth when it was much easier to hide from it.

The camera is an instrument that teaches people how to see without a camera.
—DOROTHEA LANGE

HANNAH SENESH

Poet. World War II fighter.

Determined to fight during World War II, Hannah Senesh was part of a secret British operation that parachuted into Yugoslavia. She was only twenty-two at the time. She was the only woman in the group of paratroopers.

She grew up in a nice home, just like you. She was full of personality, just like you. And she loved writing poems.

But in 1938, as Hitler rose to power and the Hungarian government started passing laws against the Jews, Hannah's classmates began spitting at the Jews.

In 1939, outraged and fearful, Hannah made her way to what is now called Israel.

But as World War II escalated and information started arriving that Hitler was killing Jews, Hannah Senesh decided she couldn't just stand there. Her mother was still in Hungary.

Hannah had to fight back.

In March 1944, the young poet became part of a small group that parachuted into Nazi-occupied Yugoslavia, with the goal of crossing into her hometown in Hungary. Their plan was to help Jews fight the Nazis and rescue those who needed help.

After three months, she finally entered Hungary. She was captured immediately.

In prison, they tried to break her. They wanted the vital radio codes that the British had trusted her with. Hannah never gave in.
They threatened her, beat her, and tortured her. She never gave in.
Even when they arrested Hannah's mother and said they'd kill her, too, Hannah Senesh never told the Nazis what they wanted to know.

In the end, they convicted her of treason. She was sent to face the firing squad.
Forever defiant, she wouldn't beg for a pardon.
She even refused the blindfold so her executioners would have to look her in the eyes.

But let me tell you right now, I didn't pick Hannah Senesh as a hero because she *died*.
I picked her because she fought.
And fought.
And fought.
That's why she'll always be remembered.

There are stars whose radiance is visible on Earth though they have long been extinct. There are people whose brilliance continues to light the world even though they are no longer among the living. These lights are particularly bright when the night is dark. They light the way for humankind.
—HANNAH SENESH

RANDY PAUSCH

Professor. Author of The Last Lecture.

A month after being told he had only three to six months left to live, Professor Randy Pausch gave his last lecture, "Really Achieving Your Childhood Dreams." But the reason millions watched online—and bought his book—was because it was never a speech about dying. It was about living.

His last lecture has been heard by millions, which is why *Time* magazine named him one of the world's most influential people.

But on the day after Randy Pausch died, his six-year-old son, Dylan, walked up to one of his father's friends and asked, "Is cancer solvable?"

His father's friend told him the truth: there was no cure for pancreatic cancer.

This clearly didn't sit well with Dylan, who relayed what his father had told him during the last few days before his death: *My dad told me I have it within me to solve problems. How could this one not be solvable?*

And that's *exactly* why Randy Pausch is so important.

On those days before he died, when millions upon millions of people were watching his lecture, Randy spent his final moments with an audience of three. His three children.

Was the message heard?

Last summer, Randy's son Dylan went to Capitol Hill. To lobby for pancreatic cancer research.

So yes, it's great when millions of people *hear* your message.

But it's far more important when even just one *acts* on it.

> *When it comes to men who are romantically interested in you, it's really simple. Just ignore everything they say and only pay attention to what they do.*
> —ADVICE RANDY PAUSCH PASSED TO HIS DAUGHTER

EXPLORER

SALLY RIDE

Astronaut. First American woman in space.

On June 18, 1983, mission specialist Sally Ride broke through the sound barrier, then the atmosphere. For 147 hours, she hovered above us all, inspiring a new generation of astronauts.

When Sally Ride was a child, her teachers used to wheel in black-and-white TVs so the students could watch the space launches.

Back then, only men could be astronauts.

Women were grounded.

Sally Ride didn't believe that.

So when NASA finally decided to accept women as astronauts,

and she saw the ad that NASA placed in the student newspaper at her college,

Sally Ride applied.

And on June 18, 1983, she became the first American woman to venture into space.

To this day, NASA has never said why she was the first woman chosen.

Some say it was because of her PhD in the field of physics.

Others say it was her physical resolve and athletic ability, which she honed as a tennis player.

And still others say it was because she was fearless.

In truth, it was probably *all* those things.

But it was also because, when she saw that ad in the newspaper, she saw an opportunity.

And grabbed it,

daring to achieve what no woman had done before.

All adventures, especially into new territory, are scary. —SALLY RIDE

BENJAMIN FRANKLIN

Founding Father. Big thinker.

The embodiment of American ingenuity, Benjamin Franklin led a military revolution—and an intellectual one.

He started as a printer.

From there, he became an author, publisher, thinker, and satirist.

He's the genius who invented

bifocals,

the lightning rod,

the Franklin stove,

a rocking chair attached by string to an overhead fan,

even the first subscription library.

But he refused to patent his famous findings, since he believed they should benefit everyone.

When he flew a silk kite—with a wire sticking up from the top, and a key attached to the base of the wet string—he helped pave the way for us to understand electricity, making him one of the most celebrated scientists in the world.

And of course, he signed—and worked on—all three of the major documents that helped establish the United States: the Declaration of Independence, the Treaty of Paris, and the U.S. Constitution.

But of all Ben Franklin's amazing attributes, his best was this:

He never forgot where he came from.

No matter how big his reputation grew, throughout his life, Franklin continued to sign his name: *B. Franklin, printer.*

He did it because Benjamin Franklin's true belief was in the power of ordinary citizens. But here's the greatest part: No one—absolutely *no one*—is ordinary.

He that can have Patience, can have what he will. —BENJAMIN FRANKLIN

Tell me and I forget. Teach me and I remember. Involve me and I learn.
—BENJAMIN FRANKLIN

WILMA RUDOLPH

Fastest woman on earth.

Although disabled by polio as a child, Wilma Rudolph went on to become the world's fastest woman, winning three Olympic gold medals.

When you're a runner, how you launch at the start of a race is vital to your success.

Wilma Rudolph had a tough launch.

Born two months premature, she weighed just four and a half pounds.
African American in Tennessee, her family was poor, and she was the twentieth of her father's twenty-two children.

When she was four, she got polio, a disease that robbed her of the use of her left leg.
When she was six, the doctors had her wearing metal leg braces.

To get to the hospital for physical therapy, her mother rode with her in the back of the segregated Greyhound bus.

When she was nine, the leg braces came off.

Soon, the girl who struggled to walk . . . began to run.

No one moved as fast.

At just sixteen, she won a bronze medal in the 1956 Olympics.
And at the age of twenty, Wilma Rudolph became the first American woman to win three gold medals in one Olympics.

Without a doubt, how you start in the race matters.
But it doesn't determine where you'll finish.

My doctors told me I would never walk again. My mother told me I would. I believed my mother.
—WILMA RUDOLPH

DOTTY RUBIN

My grandmother.

The greatest dancer and show woman on the face of the earth.

I called her "Nanny." She's my grandmother. Your great-grandmother.

And when she gave birth to my mom, the doctors told her that my mom had a disorder in her hips and that she'd never be able to walk.
Nanny took her to the House of St. Giles, one of the first hospitals in the country to deal with orthopedic care for children. They got my mom walking.

But here's what I love:
Ten, twenty, thirty, forty years later—Nanny *never* forgot what that hospital did for her.
Even when she was in her seventies and eighties and had almost no money, we'd find checks for five dollars . . . for two dollars . . . and every year she'd send a check to St. Giles.

Think about your own life.
Think of how easy it is to focus on the bad and how people have wronged you.
Nanny *never* forgot the good that she was given in this world.

Even as her life got harder—when her husband died—everyone thought she'd never recover. But she did.
And when she went blind, we thought she'd never recover. But she did.
And when she went practically deaf. Same thing.
"How you doing, Nanny?" I'd yell into her hearing aids when we went to visit on the weekends.
"I can't see anymore, darling," ninety-year-old Nanny would say. "But I can't complain."

She was wrong. She *could've* complained. She was blind and deaf and living without her beloved husband and daughter, who both were already dead.
She could've complained all day long.
But no matter how bad it got, Nanny was . . . irrepressible.
Her optimistic spirit lifted her—and therefore lifted all of us.

She came from nothing—no money. No nice house in the suburbs.
But in life, in her family, she found *everything*.

Never goodbye, darling.   —DOTTY RUBIN, who when you said "Goodbye"
                                                             would always insist on "See you later."

TERI MELTZER

My mom.

It was the worst day of my professional life.

My publisher was shutting down, and we had no idea if another publisher would take over my contract.

This was terrifying to me. I was racked with fear, feeling like I was watching my career deteriorate.

But as I shared my fears with my mother, her reaction was instantaneous: "I'd love you if you were a garbageman."

It wasn't anything she practiced. It was just her honest feelings at that moment.

To this day, *every* day that I sit down to write, I say those words to myself—"I'd love you if you were a garbageman"—soaking in the purity and selflessness of that love from my mother.

Her name was Teri Meltzer. And she's who your brother Theo is named after.

Now you'll understand how I love you.
                    —TERI MELTZER, on the birth of each of my children

Not everyone is nice like that.
    —THE RECEPTIONIST IN MY MOM'S DOCTOR'S OFFICE, when she heard that my
    mom had died from breast cancer. Always remember: the truth is what people say
                                            behind your back.

CORI FLAM MELTZER

Mother.

She's the most important hero in here.
Your mom.

When she was in fourth grade, a category-5 hurricane hit the Dominican Republic.
She was only nine years old, but Cori heard that people there were suffering.
Some people wrote checks. Others made personal donations.
Your mother's solution?
She started a club. To collect canned goods.
Soon, they were running a school-wide food drive.
Even in fourth grade, she was smart: the more people she involved, the more hurricane victims she could help.

I love that story.
And I love it because, all these years later, one of your mother's favorite expressions is this:
People don't change.

She's actually wrong.
Your mother changed me.

But.
When it comes to herself, here's what's never changed:

From high school, to Harvard, to being a lawyer for the House Judiciary Committee, to her work for inner-city schools with City Year, your mother has always loved to pick a good fight.
And it's always—*always*—the same fight:
A fight for someone else.

Best of all, there's no one—not on this entire planet—who, every single day, fights the way she fights for *you*.
She always will.

You have a strong mother, Lila.
Let it make you a strong woman.

Your Hero's photo here

Your Hero's story here . . .

Your Hero's story here . . .

Your Hero's story here . . .

_____

_____

_____

_____

_____

_____

_____

_____

_____

_____

_____

_____

_____

_____

_____

_____

_____

_____

_____

_____

_____

There are many heroes in this world. Far more than we could fit in one book. If you have a hero, please share your story with us. Your hero could be someone everyone knows or someone only you know. We'd love to hear, for instance, about the teacher or mentor who made a difference in your life.

So please send your story to:
Bradmeltzer44@gmail.com
or to
Brad Meltzer
20533 Biscayne Boulevard #371
Aventura, FL 33180

To see even more of what you can do, please visit:
www.OrdinaryPeopleChangeTheWorld.com
www.facebook.com/bradmeltzer
and
www.BradMeltzer.com

PHOTO CREDITS

Grateful acknowledgment is given to the following sources for photographs in this book:

Marie Curie: Culver Pictures Inc.; Mallory Holtman and Liz Wallace: Associated Press/Blake Wolf; Joan Ganz Cooney: Courtesy of Sesame Workshop; Audrey Hepburn: Magnum Photos/ Photographer Philippe Halsman; Helen Keller: Library of Congress, Photographer: Whitman Studio, Reproduction number: LC-USZ61-326; Christopher Reeve: James A. Parcell/*The Washington Post*/Getty Images; Carol Burnett: Library of Congress, New York World Telegram & Sun Collection, 1964; Amelia Earhart: New York *World-Telegram* and the *Sun Newspaper* Photograph Collection, Library of Congress, LC-USZ62-119130; Alex Scott: Courtesy of Alex's Lemonade Stand Foundation; Abigail Adams: Library of Congress, Reproduction number: LC-USZ62-10016; Anne Frank: Photo by Anne Frank Fonds/Anne Frank House via Getty Images; Dorothy Day: ©Bob Fitch Photo; Judy Blume: Courtesy of Judy Blume, Not for reproduction or use other than for the specific purpose of *Heroes for My Daughter*; Sacajawea: Library of Congress, Reproduction number: LC-USZ62-93141; Theodore Roosevelt: Library of Congress, Reproduction Number: LC-USZ62-39219; Julia Child: Photographer: David Marlin, Credit : National Portrait Gallery, Smithsonian Institution / Art Resource, NY, Image Reference : ART425912; Golda Meir: Associated Press , Created: 2/22/1957; Stevie Wonder: Author: Pete Souza, Date: 25 February 2009; Susan B. Anthony: Library of Congress, Photographer: S.A. Taylor, Reproduction Number: LC-USZ62-23933; Nancy G. Brinker: Courtesy of Susan G. Komen for the Cure; Clara Barton: Clara Barton National Historic Site, United States Department of the Interior, National Park Service. Photographs scanned and edited with the assistance of Volunteer Bruce Douglas; Sheila Spicer: Miami-Dade County Public Schools and HJMiami Photo; Winston Churchill: National Archives, ARC Identifier 197118; Lisa Simpson: ©2011 BONGO ENTERTAINMENT, INC. THE SIMPSONS ©&™ TWENTIETH ENTURY FOX FILM CORPORATION. ALL RIGHTS RESERVED; Eleanor Roosevelt:

ABOUT THE AUTHOR

BRAD MELTZER is the #1 *New York Times* bestselling author of *The Inner Circle*, *The Book of Fate*, and six other bestselling thrillers. He is also the host of the TV show *Brad Meltzer's Decoded* on the History Channel. He lives in Florida with his wife and three children. His sons prefer the book *Heroes for My Son*.
His daughter prefers this one.
www.BradMeltzer.com
facebook.com/bradmeltzer